POEMS

BY
BEN MAZER

THE PEN & ANVIL PRESS

BOSTON

2010

Some of these poems have appeared in *Boston Review*, *The Dark Horse*, *Filter*, *Free Verse*, *Fulcrum*, *Jacket*, *Mirage/Period(ical)*, *Poetry Calendar*, *Stand*, *Typo*, *Vallum*, *The Wolf*, and *Zoland Poetry*. "A Movie Is Available Knowledge" was printed as a letterpress broadside by Brave Men Press. "Elegy in a Windy Rain" (in a slightly different form) and "Evening" first appeared in *Johanna Poems*, published by Cy Gist Press. "The Dome" is a reconfiguration of several poems which appear in *January 2008* (Dark Sky Books). I am particularly indebted to the editors of *Fulcrum: An Annual of Poetry and Aesthetics*, where many of these poems appeared for the first time.

ISBN 978-0-9821625-4-5

Design by Zachary Bos

The Pen & Anvil Press
PO Box 15274
Boston, Massachusetts 02215
www.penandanvil.com

for Philip

Contents

The Double

I remember chiefly the warp of the curb, and time going by.
As time goes by. I remember red gray green blue brown brick
before rain or during rain. One doesn't see who is going by.
One doesn't think to see who is going by.
One sees who is going by all right, but one doesn't see who is going by.
The bright lights attract customers to the bookstore.
Seeing, chalk it up to that. The bitter looks of the booksellers,
as you leave the shop without paying. Rickety steps that will soon
be history. A ripped up paperback book with some intelligent inscriptions
in very dried out blue gray ink. Lots of dumpsters. And seagulls.
Or are they pigeons. They seem related, as the air is to the sea.
When it gets darker, or foggier, it is a really big soup
of souls, works of art, time tables, the hour before dinner,
theatrical enterprise, memories of things never happened, warnings
spoken in a voice familiar, a keen and quickened sense
of possibility glimpsed through windows.
Handbills, whatever to mark the passing time. And sleep.
I know it is good when the good of it is not noticed.
It is something you try to tell someone privately in a room
where the light is broken in October. Your sense of time
is the source of your charm with strangers,
who would accept you anyways.
Nora Laudani was the best actress in our elementary school.
One felt she was a great lady at seventeen.
The tragic view of ice skating frightens us
at night in winter. In a soup you never know
what you'll run into next. All the ingredients repeat,
but you encounter some of them for the first time. Strangers
turn out to be people you know later on. Sometimes even dead people's
lives are only a stone's throw away from your own. First you heard of them,
or heard someone speaking like them. Generations of birds

are some kind of commentary on it. People who moved out precede you.
If your cousins are playing football on the lawn, then somebody else's
        cousins
played football on the lawn. You try to imagine them when you are alone.
It is interesting that you are the only one on the street. Time as a movie.
When you are walking everything is moving. It kind of reaches out at you,
as if inviting you to stop and visit with it,
as if having a particular story to tell.
You can't keep your mind on the story it has to tell.
But some of the things you're reminded of *are* the story it's telling you.
They are too much like other things you've heard about. Their advantage is
the hands of trees think you want to pick them. They kind of don't want you
        to go inside,
but they want you to know that something's going on in there.
I am constantly reminded of George Washington
when I look in at the shapes of windows. Social courtesy looms large,
and throws lavish parties. Its savage powers are pride's poster.
There is a kind of perpetual removal in a spiral.
The case of a person who is very rapidly assessing several objects at once.
He either has a machine to do this for him, or recognizes value.
I was thinking of the moon along the Wabash.
In April white scroll-work admires magnolias.
The white picket fence is and has always been intense.
After a while Walt Whitman doesn't come again, but is in fact receding.
Snow has a very conspiratorial hush in circumstances similar to these.
One lets a real good laugh out. The universe seems to yield a little bit for
        the laugh.
The stars pass the houses more quickly than you do.
Your race is the measure of time.
Your race is the meaning of time.
That makes you laugh. After all it looks like it is just you
and pavement that is going nowhere. The houses in back lots between
        houses

raise their hats in your hopes until you see them as dead wood,
and begin to get thoughts related to the inception of maps.
This's binary coordinate is sleep.
Often it is much better than I am describing.
Now let it be a lens through which we look at the city
on a long drive at night, with its feeling of going to a doctor.
Shy shared moments between the wind and the palmetto,
and a feeling of having been missed by only ten or twenty years.
Something which is not wholly love and only abstractly journalism.
In the luggage department palmettos are on empty. The steps
are your best bet. Try prickly! Past the doorbell
lies the paradise for which you are kicking yourself.

Rhapsody on a Winter Night

The closed world adumbrates the snow.
Midnight deciphers pillows at the window.
Though it was several months ago,
in dead of winter, nothing knows or shows
where the requested intimacy goes.
The silent isolated frames
of meditation have dispersed with names.
The couches crouch in feeble poses,
incognizant of roses.

Death and Minstrelsy

"Our references have all aged a little
as we were looking at them, not noticing."
– John Ashbery

That hulking rooftop like a leviathan
still unexpectedly sails into view,
its byzantine tilework faded red and grey
like boxes within boxes visible from the sea,
at summer's start eluding the goswogii.
Woodberry's copy of his life of Poe
emerges from the flood, a constancy
that nobody will buy year after year.
Poe was born in Boston. In aught nine
Bruce Rogers did the job and Eliot
did shameful things that never will be known
on out of town trips. Something in the fog
grins like a skeleton beneath the cracked
continuity of what seemed like time.
Fall is spring-like. The fresh violins
of new arrangements lift the tortured heart
to hope, reflected light, the heart laid bare.
Poems are but evidence of poetry.
Mysterious kitchens you shall search them all—
and choose your death at sea by thirty-three.
And once in winter heard the Archduke Trio
performed by friends in the conservatory.
Although I am only a moderate admirer
of your poetry, there is not a single other
contemporary poet who I do admire.
The museum closes in a timeless wave
of unutterable rhythms, lashed by rain.

The sea's maw beckons to the life it spawned.
The white sheen of a sun pierced spray of fog
as we drop down the hill to the cliff's edge
pierces the crowd out of time's slow parade
that hits us like old music or a dream,
billowing out between their stupored legs,
the hot dog zeppelins and powder flags,
as if unseeable, but the grey ghost
of that hellion rowing with an iron crowbar
peers out through banjo chinks in the ragtime
that's near but sounds as if it's far away,
the certainty of death past the breakers.

The Long Wharf

It takes awhile to walk through the long wharf
which is enclosed against the elements.
Purveying the connecting properties
to the new lease, our party sauntered there,
in the bright glare of light deflecting night,
the Chinaman, the Frenchman and the Swede
(each in a pressed suit, just off an airplane,
and eager to get back to the hotel,
to sink in privacy into a drink
in a bright glare of light deflecting night),
their uninformed eyes taking little care
(the tour was peppered with such agent's talk
as never hesitates in its intent,
was not designed for one to really look),
while the collector of fine bric-a-brac
who counted millions in the warehoused goods
rubbed off a bit of calculating pride
on objects he could not commit to sell,
stealthy foundations of his capital:
each type of bottle from each type of year,
each printed calendar that was produced,
all manufactured products, everything
preserved unopened in its packaging
just as it was when joie de vivre was king
(the Englishwoman served him to this end,
looking upon him as upon a friend).
The long wharf was unstable in the wind.
We didn't realize it was a wharf
we had come through, but at the end of it
a weather-rotted window peered out on
the ocean, we could see how far we'd come

held up above the sea by massive beams,
a long way out, and swaying in the wind
with little place to walk on the loose floor.

I thought of falling out into the sea.
The ocean is blue, but many shades of blue
and white and green, and black and grey, combined
in motion, rising towards us on a page
behind which light hides echoes of nothing.
Nothing is all we know of what is there.
It seems so heavy, heavier than dreams,
as deep as dreams would ever think to go,
in the black murky movement that's not there.
What ever comes behind has come before
and either is or has or hasn't been,
it's not for us to say. If we're not here,
historically, life is happening elsewhere.
All is a paradigm, the diver's bow
is nothing if not everything we know.
I want to turn the page. I am afraid
of what is out there, the horizon, ships—
depthless darkness, uncertain vantages.
I pulled back from the wind as from a nail,
and turned to go. There on some long tables
(I had been squeezed between them and the wall
when I had had my vision of my fall)
whose sides were built up so that they were bins
I saw enormous quantities of slips
of paper, very thin, filed in long rows.
I opened one to see what slips they were.
Upon each one, and now I saw the ships
that must have been as real as you or I,
the name recorded of each voyager

transgressing the horizon on a ship
who entered here, each entry had a slip—
a continent of ghosts had landed here,
thick on the tables, only the fog moved
and the long wharf stayed up and swayed in place.

Second Rhapsody on a Winter Night

[Variations on a Winter Night]

I

Night extends opacities
of being and of consciousness.
Physical vacuities.

Beneath the porcelain awake
tidal waves of other lives
and unburied memory.

The evening hour's to and fro,
time's thick repercussions bloom
(the hour of the small meeting).

Landscape and emotion rains.
Consciousness and being drains.
And toy soldiers storm the seas.

II

Tangled prospects of the trees.
Perspectives' difficulties.

Scenery that no one sees.
Perpetual vacuities.

Amid it all an ancient roar,
a disciplinary whisper.

A confidence of alcoves,
a confidence of loves.

And the disconnected spires,
and the disembodied towers.

The splintered multiplicity
of bare branches of a tree.
Scenery that no one sees.
The row of deserted balconies.
(A light comes on between the trees
and flickers from within a room.)
The tangled vacuities
of shade and shape
of shape and shade.
The tomorrow that's prepared.

Footprints through pure forms of snow
sink like thought into shadow.
Snow that's piled on barriers,
motionless fragments of verse.

And the soul shrinks in the wood
far from what is understood.

(The lights come on between the trees.)

And the toy soldiers storm the seas.

Tangled prospects of the trees.
Perspectives' difficulties.

And the sleeping melodies

of motionless uncertainties.
And the sleeping melodies
of abandoned vacancies.
And the sleeping melodies
of forms and structures without cease.
And the sleeping melodies
of abandoned centuries.
And the streetlight on the street,
the absent tread of absent feet.

And the soul shrinks in the wood
far from what is understood.

(And flickers from within a room
where I shall neither go nor come.)
The bold indifference of the moon
settles on a window pane.
And tomorrow is prepared
in the darkness without word.
As darkness with symphonic form
agitates the empty room.
As stillness with symphonic form
agitates the lifeless room.
And tomorrow is prepared
in the hall without a sound.
Wordlessly as memory.
Wordlessly as memory
through the outer room is wound.
(The present and the future bound.)
As silence with symphonic form
agitates the sleepless room.
And tomorrow is prepared.
And tomorrow is prepared,

and the future is secured
(though the present is obscured).
And the world itself is tired.
Language by itself is bored.
And tomorrow is required.
And the morning is prepared.

Consciousness and being drains.
Landscape and emotion rains.

Ancestral resonances freeze.
And the toy soldiers storm the seas.

The Dome

I

I hunt the houses where you left your mark
in wooden objects and paint surfaces
for him or her. The hesitating dark
unveils your love in words that never cease
illuminating rooms that we have left
or you left earlier, replaying scenes
where secrets whisper louder and arrest
the underground oblivion of our dreams.
Because you put a gun to love my love
dies full of bullets under the plane tree.
You are laughing almost from above
at nothing really, what we choose to see
because you meant in doing what you did
the full extent of love before you died.

II

Dear Miss Poe, please grow your hair long
and spend your furlough prinking by the furlong,
cast honey pelts of doubt into the dong
of slinking evening. Let true love be wrong
and hang from cornices of misspent song.
Invent in traffic of your veins my trick
of listening before the voice's prick.
Oppose the throng of nothing in the tick
of painted evening. Languish in the kick
of sundry calendars besprinkling time.

III

March evaporates the granite rains
along the rooftops, where nothing detains
the idle moonlight peeking through the clouds,
and by the stellar axis of their shrouds
climbs down enormous branches of a tree
a muslin corner of the library
glimpses, where unfettered in the wind
the new year pricks the hearing of the blind,
and passes through demented promises
although it is not yet the time for kisses.

IV

Buds. Ice. Pines. Windows. Babes. New year.
Elephant. Window seat. Octagonal. Reflection.
Silence. Shuddering. Hammering. Welcoming.
Division. Fragmentation. Peace. Visitor.
Township. Echoing. Report. Christening.
Baptism. Recollection of foretelling.
Schism. Prism. Arrival. Windless current.
Opportunity. Decision. Incantation. Invitation.
Darkness. Listening. Loosening. Lightening.
There is nothing like it. It is not what is it.
You know how I want you to know.

V

Her cautiousness he painted blue
so she could see it from the window
covered over with a blue haze
that stumped the streetlight.
Then she was his visitor
and never came again to say
the porticoes across the street
were dappled in the winter moon.
These indexes of where they stood
a crux for nothing, reminded
the armchair where to begin
consternating from the floor.

VI

A leaf below the crust again
replete bodacious gathering
investing whom to bloom within
expostulating medicine
to how whoever whom so be
retarded in the water crest
impervious beyond the sea.

VII

Not the carpet, the floor.
At linespread, under talk
of Oedespeu, weird spew
word of Atlantic convo-
lutions meant to disfigure
the history lesson that had
come to pass. On the dawn
the effacive what is it
of his plans turned into
our older windowshade
of welcome, society
of word in print, his plan.
Semi-retiring the flashing
colors of his hurdles bit
into and slowly ate away
our resolve. He had brought
messages from other cities
to turn us under into our
own cessation, but for us.

VIII

The Solway was their own particular hell,
each time the station loomed over the train
they reinitiated marriage vows
and went directly to the little steeple
where they had first made love, where you could see
his people's land. His friend's new death
had made the little mountain side curves steeper
and all the low tomatoes in the dark

feared for the coming time, the giant's step.
His son drew maps on blank white sheets of paper
that showed the drills and where the aircraft landed.
Chopin ruffled evening and the wine
drew scarlet patterns on the guests who dined.
I wish I had a photo of that day
to capture the brink of that society.
All we can now do is relive
the secret satisfactions of their love.

IX

The stars are glittering into the heaven
when you arrive. The sofa coverlets
lowered into place by bluebirds. A Ming vase
entertaining echoes reminds you of
where you have been. A magnolia grove
shuttered into shadow by the evening.
Gossamer epaulets of telling time
hang from your motion. Snapping fans
elucidate the view of match boxes.
Unguent breath requires a text of song.
A plectrum scattered at the old piano.

The Microfilm City

The pressure of expression gave us this:
a microfilm city. Poring through the ads
of every daily, working through the tunnel
of eight years ('38 through '47)
I saw the streets, snow-covered and slush-covered
(and the boudoirs, the intimate warm ladies
whose faces the historical erases,
but for a moment dressed by silk distinctions
in blackened tones of conversation
presuming or presumed by libraries
of time tables, advertisements and fiction,
manuals for being of one's time
with the conviction, the presupposition
of the preceding hours, for a dime),
and followed the worn-out routes of absent schedules
to meet with gestures circumscribing feeling,
contractual constructions, idioms of meaning
reduced to desolation, unimpeding,
attend events on which there is no bearing,
which have no alternatives for repairing,
if these be ghosts, alive with warmth and feeling.
And what, I ask, tonight will they be wearing?
And where will my own ghosts go, these friends I'm nearing . . .

(And such a face will pin me with its meaning.)

(And warm warm breasts that have no need for feeling,
portraiture depending from another ceiling.)

The North

a and b triangulate c and d
in the northern corner, yellow and orange
triangulate red and green beneath the brown
august of autumn, and the corner room
broods upon return, end of the street
shuttered by wishes, renounced over dinner.
b and c invite blue, introduce
the relevant stranger to the old alcove,
the eternal hallway, making it internal
so the past becomes the future, the present past,
the inevitable obsolescent exemplar.

Crushed Rains

"I wonder if it is too late or soon
For the resolution that our lives demand."
— The March Hare

When all red satin monkeys sleep on trains,
emotions recollecting absent rains,
and sapphire blue eyes streaked with the rains,
whose absence I am left with for my pains,

wondering what's become of failed romances,
missed opportunities, lost chances,
now twenty years of dinners and of dances,
the felt but never undertaken stances,

presents no anniversary celebrates,
having no substance to become the past,
no nodding or caressing self-assurances,
no winking or affirming circumstances,

will yet too late too suddenly emerge
signs of regret vicissitudes discourage.

Stieglitz

Not the sheer beauty of perpetual snow,
nor the exactitude of transience,
but the required insolence of framing
the inexplicable.

The Exile

I was handled by the handler's handler
someone (I know who) had sent me to.
A mountain zephyr blew the sunlight cold.
I read the little village paper backwards
and nibbled at my ham. Coffee is birth.
I was surprised to see how things had changed
since I first dreamed I came here long ago.
The villagers were lobbying new plans,
who had been immigrants before the snow.
I was among the first to try the new
cuisine, the classless restaurant.
In the best house I recognized my host,
and he who had fulfilled a noble life
exhibited no need for conversation.
Then I was swept up in the exultation
of thousands of revelers' descent to hell.

Orient Heights

Orient heights the sole star blessed
motion against motion movement against movement
to the one house buried in the rest
no one sees me but an old man
I've come to use drunk in his playroom
sole star blessed and a blank page
divided between the world as we know it
the world as we saw it and a blank page
and all the rest Orient heights

While You Were Watching Richard Harris

Then or now, the eye let on the storm.
Winks of knowing, dead before alive.
Simple patter, nothing to write home.
British wishes, twentieth century jive.

An ape's greek profile, and the grainy slosh
of primary dimensions. Tragedy
is just a face, enslavement's kitchenette.
This has the mortal sound of tragic ease.

The awkward awful listenerless blown
enjambments. Dreadful paraphrase. Unshown!
Escapes amazement. Notches on recall
the figurement of the Platonic wall.

Yet, lacking mores, nothing to exhume.
As if from rooftops lengthening to bloom.

Cambria 1943

The moon is full over Australia—
The Cambrian dawn assuages, tidal rage
of cloud and zodiac sweeping the page
of summer's welter, shimmer without shelter.
The dawns invade and raid the shell and splinter
splitting time, foretold by no one, splayed
in the opposing and eventual sun.
Trestled tufted at the top of timber
the highs unload and the perspectives limber
into the loan of lenient amber looking
for words that aren't words, where space retards
the person, fixing the star fires,
where all is shale and shell and blue white-dyed.

Before Us

i.m. Frank Parker

Lowell winning the Pulitzer in 1947...
Pushing ecstatic through the darkening crowd...
the newspapers not yet lifted, fish and corn
wrapped by the flashing grocer, millennial...
weighed in two scales by his hurt, flashing eyes...
a seething margin, bustling with friends
and lovers, trinket-shaking sky, to die...
how can they tell us what they didn't know?
Logical types the century pressed white...
rounding the corner of each first familiar
tombstone or commemorative stone
cut in the image of the training sailor...
homecoming, whether on the edge of home.
Writing is fighting in the Christ-whale's eyes.

The Big House

Spring draws archival colors, brief and brittle
as celluloid, its technicolor process
too early for man, too late for a bright rebuttal,
along dirt roads, easing out travellers' faces.
Love swings in gates, shines in new coats of white,
tuning up breezes, whistling branches and collars,
lighting out birds, examining concrete
as far as the eye can see, exploding flowers.
Bringing petitions for a timely pardon,
willing to go on record if it might save,
only true love can influence the warden.
"I'm giving the orders now. We're crashing out."
Living the rest of my days the way he might have,
out of the prison now, I'll write about it.

Blackbirds

Not yet the shocking end of the ballet
with stumps and bleeding as the poet draws,
anticipated seated for the play
at eight o'clock, the eastern ice plain thaws
and the short wireless signal decays
amid the sound of thundering applause
where the bride meets the bridegroom and the maze
of teacups subjugated to the cause
of the new Europe suffers by the way,
the oldest infancy surrounds the tower
and the homecoming ocean at that hour
flies with the blackbirds, languishing to pay
the majestic masticating jaws
of memory, all that the war allows.

Evening

Coming in the vastly later
like a time we had prepared
as if the stars invented dinner
or the evening had been cleared
by sheer invention of another
long before the deal was queered
we stepped into the times of tables
and the primes of motor cars
waiting for us as in fables
under the invented stars
and the transience of those times
were intimately just for us
a resurrection history climbs
to catch an after dinner bus
while some absent early other
shone to rankle and to bother.

A Movie Is Available Knowledge

A movie is available knowledge,
interdisciplinary garb, insane voices
uttering knowledge. Too much fun
remembers. On the hill the balcony
is windy. Better be said. Nothing
recommends the bluebirds. Better
the west wind. Remembers the ghosts love.
I am troubled by experience.

The high hedges languish the ocean.
Here it is eves then. Notion
knows no no. The North Star
freezes the ship's light like fire
over the white surf. The black death
roars silence, over the white sands.

EVEN AS WE SPEAK

THE MOVIES. HOME LIFE. CHILDHOOD. PAST CENTURIES.
FACES AND TALK. PAINTINGS AND SENSATIONS.
STUBBORN SHYNESS. BRIGHTBIRDS FLOWERING
MORNING. ORSON WELLES. CITIZEN KANE.
MAGNIFICENT AMBERSONS. TREE GROWS IN BROOKLYN.
DAVID COPPERFIELD. TREASURE ISLAND. THE KID.
ORPHANS. POPPY. MISTAKEN IDENTITY. LIGHT IN THE
HALLWAY. ROSES OF DAWNING OVER THE SHOULDER.
POE. POE. NOT EVEN DARKNESS. NEVER GIVE A SUCKER
AN EVEN BREAK. AND THERE IS NO TIME, NO TIME. NO.
WITH THE CAT HOWLING TO BE LET IN. NO NEED TO
WRITE. ONLY THIS WHAT I'M TELLING YOU. TELLING
MYSELF. THERE IS A BEGINNING TO ALL THIS. AN
OCCASION. SCOTTISH BAGPIPES ARE ITS EQUIVALENT,
BUT IT BEAMS DOWN IN SPECKLED LIGHTS. SPOKEN
LIGHTS. I WOULDN'T SAY. GOAT LIGHT. SAWDUST.
WINDMILL. GATHERING. OR SILENCE OF TEARS, LIKE
RAIN ON THE HILL STREET, HOVERING OVER THE
GREEN GRASS, SILENCE OF NEIGHBORS, SILENCE OF
BEETHOVEN. CHARLIE'S SALOON. PASTRAMI, CORNED
BEEF, ROOTBEER AND A PICKLE. FRENCH FRIES. MOM
AND DAD. SISTER. NIGHT OUT. THE STRANGE SUNRISE,
OR WAS IT SUNSET, COVERED OVER THE TEAR OF THE
EYES OF THE CHILD. ONE EVENING IN A DECADE. IN THE
TRAFFIC TRUCKED OUT OVER THE MOMENT. OVER THE
BRIDGE AND THE TRAFFIC AND THE WEATHER OF THE
MOMENT. WHERE THE SHADOWS GRIND INTO A COLOR
THAT ONLY YOU AND GOD SEE, OR ONLY YOU SEE, BUT
IF GOD SEES IT, OR IT IS LIKE WHAT OTHER PEOPLE SEE,
THEN IT IS AS IF IT WERE RECORDED IN A CALENDAR,
BROADCAST, TRANSCRIPT OR PERPETUAL TRIBUNE IN

THE STADIUM OF EXISTENCE.

WOULD FRAME A GATHERING. NOT JUST THE
LIGHTNESS OF STEP IN ANOTHER COUNTRY, NEARER
THE EQUATOR. ABSENCE OF SHADOW. THE OLD STORY.
COME TO TOO LATE, OR JUST ON TIME. SUN LIKE A
NEWSPAPER, TURNING THE LEAF OF DAY. A SPOT OF
WALL, IN THE NORTH. CHARITY OF STRANGERS, FRIENDS
OF FATHER'S. VOLUMES ON THE SHELF. SHADOW
VARNISHING AN ORANGE WALL. BREAST FULL OF
SHADOWS. SLICING MEMORIES. DISTENSIONS. A LAMP'S
WORTH OF PUNISHED. THE LAMP'S WORD.

IT IS THE SEA'S HIGH POSTING OF NUMBERS OVER THE
CRITIQUED CONTEST OF THE IDENTITY, WHERE THE
SHADOW OF SHADOWS GATHERS. WHERE THE PINES
ARE EQUIVALENT TO ARRIVAL, OR WHAT IS TOLD IN
SUNLIGHT FALLS, WHERE IT IS SPOKEN, TO BE TOLD
AGAIN OR FOLD INTO MEMORY. GRETEL ON THE
DOORSTEP. THE GINGERBREAD HOUSE. THE OTHER
REALITY ENTERED BY MIRRORS. SHE ENTERED THE
ROOM. THE WORLD TURNS. NUMBERS ARE POSTED OVER
THE OCEAN.

ANGELS KNEW THAT THIS WAS GOING TO HAPPEN.
RELATIVES TELL IT AND IT HAPPENS AGAIN. NOT ONLY
THAT IT UNFOLDED IN CHRIST'S ARMS LIKE A CRADLE.
NO BUT THAT IT IS MARKED IN FORETELLING LIKE A
NEWSPAPER. WINDY RADIO RAIN. ECHOES LIKE DREAMS,
THINGS THEY ARE TELLING, TRYING TO RETURN TO.
HOUSE OUT OVER THE OCEAN. FRIEND OF DAUGHTER,
DAUGHTER OF FRIEND. SAME AGE IN CHILDHOOD.
WHAT HAPPENS WHEN NO ONE IS AROUND. QUIZ YOU

TO TELL ME. MIND NOT TO SPEAK. CROSSWORD
PUZZLE'S. UNCLE'S ROOM. WHERE THEY KEPT THE
MAGAZINES. THE COOL TABLE WHERE HE KEPT HIS
TRAY. THE LONG VOLUMES OF BREEZE IN HIS ROOM'S
KEEPING.

BUT TO HAVE A FRAME, LIKE GEORGE WASHINGTON, OR
LEONARD LEON. NOT BAD A DAD'S FRIEND'S VISIT. PUT
THIS ON A FOOTING. TABLE SEMBLANCE.
GRANDFATHERLY RESEMBLANCE. PHONING THE
PICTURE. STEPS OF GREEN ICE. TUMBLERS OF MARBLE.
CRESCENTS OF GLASS. MILK OF MOONLIGHT. AFTER
THE SLEEPING. OUT WITH THE STARS. LOOSE FROM THE
PAINTING. THE HOUR AND ANGUISH OF SLEEPING.
RESENTFUL OF THE LEFT OVER. IMAGINING THE SILENT.
THE UNMANNED WATERING BUCKET. A NEED FOR WHAT
ISN'T WATCHED OVER. A REQUEST THE SILENCE
FULFILLS.

BACK IN THE CITY THE DAY TURNED LIKE A CALENDAR,
PEOPLE STARING IN GROUPS, TURNING, STARTING UP
THE STAIRS, TIME OF DAY, WATCHED OVER LIKE A HAWK,
OR NOT WATCHED, DRIFTING, SIFTING LIFTING INTO
THE NOT EVEN NOTICED, NOTHING TO WATCH. DIDN'T
LIKE THAT LAST. A WOMAN WAITING BY THE WINDOW,
EACH AND LAST. AND THE MUSIC OF HER WAITING
EACH MINUTE OF THE YEAR. THE WAY IT HAPPENED
BEFORE, CARVED ON THE EMBLEM INSIDE OF HER
WAITING. BIRDS SLEEPING IN HER SILENCE. ROTARY
POSITION OF HER CONSIDERATION. AFTER THE FACT.
HOW THIS STARTED. ITS ANTITHESIS. THE LOCK ON THE
WALL. THE GUEST ROOM. THE DEN WITH THE SOFA BED.
THE DRAWER WITH THE LOVE LETTERS. THE

COMMEMORATIVE MATCHES. THE TELEVISION
LISTINGS, THOSE SCANNED AND THOSE NOT SCANNED.
THOSE SCANNED STABLE IN THE AIR LIKE RAIN ON THE
STREET. THE HIDDEN LISTENINGS OF THE CHOCOLATE
BOXES. THE USED AND USED AND USED PULLOVERS. THE
TIME BEFORE, WHEN THE LAST GUEST. THE LITTLE
TOWELS LIKE HOTEL'S. BETTER SOAP THAN AT HOME.
MARBLE TILES THAT SECRETS HANDED OVER. NAKED
FRIENDS. DRESSED WHEN YOU SEE THEM. LAUGHING
AND SCRUBBING. REFLECTED IN RINSE WATER AND
BUBBLES. TIME'S REFLECTION. DRACULA AT THE HOTEL.
SCARED TO WALK IN THE HALL. TEAR THINGS UP,
KNOCK THINGS OVER. PUT THINGS BACK IN THEIR
PLACE. UNMARKED BUT TOUCHED. LIKE THE NOSE IS BY
SMELL. IGNITED IN MOONLIGHT. THE STREET'S SECRET.
THE CITY FLOWING OVER THE SLEEPING, OVER THE
WAKING. PARTICULARS OF PRINT. SINCE THE 1930S. NOT
JUST TO BE SEPARATE IN THE NIGHT. THE NIGHT A
SEPARATE CITY FROM HISTORY. THE NIGHT A SEPARATE
CITY. THE SEPARATE NIGHT. THE NIGHT A SEPARATE
CITY FROM THE NIGHT. NO TELLING WHY HER
SECRETARY. GO ON AND ON AND ON AND TELLING.
FLOWERS WHAT DONE BEFORE. TO REMEMBER. AS IF
REMEMBERED. TELLING AND TELLING FLOWERS AND
FLOWERS. WHAT HER VOICE SPOKE. THE SILENCE
AFTER. AFTER THE TELLING. THE SILENCE OF NEVER
BEFORE. SLEEPING AND WAKING BELONGING TO THE
SILENCE. SCENARIOS ALL WORKED OUT. PERFECT
BRUSHSTROKE TO THE TELLING. GOOD AS BEFORE. TO
BE DISCOVERED AGAIN. A GIRL I DREAMED OF. DEAD
AND PAST. WAS IT THE VISIT TO THE AUTHOR'S HOUSE?
WHY DID THE BROOKS WIND LIKE CLOCKWORK,
FILLING HER TALK?

SPROUTING UP PAST THE LAWN. FRIENDLY ENOUGH FOR
A VISIT. TIRED OF WALKING. A CERTAIN WAY OF TALKING.
GROWING IN THE LIGHT. SNUFFLES OF LAUGHTER.
SMILES DRIPPING SILENCE. A RIGID GATHERING OF
INARTICULABLE ASSENT. UNHESITATING
ANNOUNCEMENT. A VEIL OF WAITING, EARLY ON THE
FLOWERS. THE SHIPS POURING IN WHILE IT IS STILL
MORNING. GOING TO SEE THE QUEEN. THE PEOPLE
STOPPING. RAIN STARTLING THE IMAGINATION. SENSE
OF THE FAMILIAR. WAYS OF TREES AROUND THE HOURS.
PROMISES OF THE CONTROL TOWER. THE UNIFORM'S
FLOWING FLAGS. THE BUGLE OF HISTORY, BLOWING
AGAIN. ATTITUDES REFLECTED LIKE CHARCOAL IN THE
ETHER. A WINNOWING DOWN OF WILLINGNESS. A
PERIODIC PROPOSAL. DOWN WITH THE BILLBOARDS.
TOLD YOU I DIDN'T. NEWS FOR DEAD SOLDIERS. WOULD
HAVE BEEN PROUD OF. TIME TO REVISIT WHAT WAS
SEEN ONCE. WHAT WOULD HAVE BEEN BETTER.
ROASTED CHESTNUTS. THE TRAIL OF THE PARTICULAR.
THIS TIME LAST YEAR. PILES AND PILES OF CARS TO THE
SUN. THE STRANDED BEACH. AND THE YEAR AT THE
EDGE OF THE HEAVENS. THE SEPARABLE MOMENT OF
CHRIST.

OUTLINES OF WORDS LIKE ROCK. THE POET'S HOUSE.
THE PERIODIC BREATH. THE STRANGER VISITING.
VICTORIA IN VICTORIA IN VICTORIA IN VICTORIA.

PEANUT BUTTER. ARRIVAL OF HORSES. THE FRACTURED
MOMENT. TURNING AND NEIGHING. FLOWERS AND
MANURE. A STIFF SMELL OF LEATHER AND HORSES,
WOODCHIPS AND DEW. THE PLEDGE OF THE FOUNTAIN.

THE INALIENABLE SCENE. BRASS MEMORIES BEFORE
THEY HAPPEN. THE LONG CALL OF THE PREDICTABLE.
THE INTIMATE HUMILITY OF THE SINGULAR. EUPHORIA
AT NOT BEING NOTICED, AT WHAT IS MISSED. THOSE
HERE BEFORE YOU, WHAT CAME BEFORE THEM. A
DRAWING OUT OF INFERENCES, POSITIONING OF DEALS.
THE MADE UP CONCLUSIONS IN THE STAGED
APPOINTMENTS. THE NEVER TOLD. PARTERS REUNITED.
THE LONG CLOSURE OF COMMITMENTS. THE BRIEF
MARKET OF PROPOSALS. THE AWAKENING INTEREST IN
THE OBSOLETE. EXTENDED ACCOMODATIONS FOR THE
RESURRECTED. A COMMON CIVILITY FOR THE
RECOGNIZED AND ATTENDED. REWARDS FOR
IMITATION. MEMBERSHIP TO THE SUFFICIENTLY
REGARDED. NO NEED TO INDEX THE PIOUSLY
SUGGESTED. A RAIN OF MAGNOLIAS, BLOWN CHERRY
BLOSSOMS. THE INFERENCE OF THE STATIC. RITUALS OF
RETENTION. OFFICES OF RETREAT. OBJECTS OF
HESITATION. FORMS WHICH REPEAT, ECHO ONE
ANOTHER IN RECOGNITION. HOLY IMAGES OF UNBORN
SPEECH. GENERATIONS OF PEOPLE BURIED IN RAIN. THE
FIRST TELLING. THE FIRST WORD. SHAPED LIKE AN
EAGLE. STILL IN ITS FOOTING. MOUNTAINS OF
WHITENESS. OVER THE MOUNTAINS. INTO THE PARLOR.
STILL ON THE SHELF. TALK WON'T UPSET IT. RAISE IT,
EVOKE IT, JUST FOR A MOMENT. ENOUGH THAT WHAT IS
IT PROCLAIM ITS SMALL KINGDOM, IN LIEU OF THE
REST. AT LAST THE GRIM TEMPLE, OF TELLING AND
DARKNESS. THE SHROUD OF THE HANDS. THE SHADOW
OF THE VOICE. THE CLOSED OFF WORLD, BEYOND THE
ROOM. THE ICY STILLNESS OF THE REVISIT. WORDS
THAT WILL DIE ALONE HERE. FEELINGS TO PUT AWAY
WITH FRIENDS. THE GRAPPLE AND GRAVEL OF PEAT

37

AND STRAIT. THE WARM CEMENT IN THE COOL WIND.
DECLARATIONS TO LIVE BY. A BETTER FEELING. THE
WORLD TO VISIT, TO SEE AGAIN. IN ALL ITS GLORY, SAME
AS EVER. THE PERFECT DEPARTURE OF THE NEW BORN.

BUT TO BEGIN WITH ENTERTAINMENT. THE MYSTERY
OF THE CLOSED DRAWERS. THE PAINTINGS AND THE
MARBLE FIGURES DIVIDING UP THE MINUTES, THE HALL
OF MIRRORS. THE COOK'S WORDS. THE ARRIVAL OF THE
GARDENER. THOUSANDS OF MINUTES SCATTERED
THROUGHOUT THE MAGNOLIA BLOSSOMS. THE CHAIN
OF REFLECTIONS. THE WISTFUL WHAT IS IT
WHISPERING ON THE EDGE OF LACK OF INTEREST. THE
MOTIF TELLING AGAIN WHAT IT IS TELLING, HAS BEEN
TELLING. PERMISSION FOR THE PRESENT TO BE
FAMILIAR. AT LAST NO DIFFERENCE. SENSATION AND
IDEAS ONE. STEPPING INTO ROLES IN THE
IMAGINATION, IN THE DEMONSTRABLE INHERITANCE.
NOT TO REMEMBER. TOO COOL, TOO ORIGINAL FOR
TELLING. PERFECT FOR KNOWING. ENTIRELY INCIPIENT.
NAME LIKE A CHAIN. A RING OF BLUEBELLS AND POSIES.
BLESSING THE CRONE'S REFRAIN. AND TIRED IN IT,
EATEN BY THE WORLD, AND BY THE DARKNESS
SWIMMING BENEATH IT, DARKNESS OF OLD MUSEUMS,
IMITATIONS OF REPRODUCTIVE THOUGHTS IN
ISOLATION. THE LANGUAGE FOR IT IS IDLE BUT
SPECIFIC, REDUCED TO CALLINGS FORTH OF SELECTIVE
LORE AND IMPEDING OUTLINES. THE SMELL AND THE
DARK OUTLINE REVISIT RAIN AS RECENTLY IT'S MAPPED
IN A SIDELONG REVERENCE FOR THE CITIES IN SHIELD'S
CREASES. LIVES MORE NOW IT IS NO MORE. ALSO NO
IMITATION THOUGH REPEATED IN CONVERSATION
FLOCKS THROUGHOUT THE HALLWAY (AND THE FAR

ALARM HAILS STILL FROM THE TOWER) WHERE IN
ANOTHER YEAR WE MET AGAIN. I DID NOT VISIT YOU TO
SEE ANOTHER, BUT CAME BECAUSE I WAS HERE. I LEAVE
YOU AS I FIND YOU. HAYSTACKS AND WINDMILLS.
BARRELS AND ASH. NO PROVOCATION SERVICES THIS. IN
THE TOWN PRICES ARE WORDS, NUMBERS CLIMBING IN
THE POCKET. AVAILABLE COLORS FOR AGREEING WITH
FLAGS AND THE CHARACTER OF A MOMENT. CHEAP
MAGAZINES. STOLEN KNICK KNACKS. NEWSPAPER
UNDER THINGS. DISMAY OF ORDER. CLOUDS COWS
MOTORING BEHIND THE ACTION, IN THE PRESENT OF
DAY, FILLED WITH REJOINDERS, PENCILS OF PAPER,
WHAT YOU WANTED IT TO BE, TOO LATE TO FIND YOU.
NOT WHAT IT IS ABOUT, BUT HOW IT GOT THERE,
REASON TO TALK ABOUT IT, STAGE OF ADVANCEMENT,
GOVERNMENT FUNDING FOR MEMORIES CAST OVER
THE NORTH OF TOWN. WELCOME PROGRESS. THAT I
CAN FIND YOU AT THE END OF ALL THIS. COURAGEOUS
TO FACE IT. FAMILIAR WITH THE TERRAIN. I TELL IT AS
IF IT WERE HAPPENING, WHERE IT HAPPENS ONCE
ONLY, IN ANY DREAM OF BEING LOST IN A FOREIGN
COUNTRY WHICH LOOKS FAMILIAR. THE DEAD ARE
WITH YOU. BRINGING NO SUITS. THIS HOLY SANCTIFIED
GROUND BLESSED THEY WERE BE HERE, NO CARDINAL
POINT. DEVICE STAMPED GIVE ANOTHER CENTURY OR
TWO TO REACH ITS EMISSARY. SIMPLE DEVOTION IS THE
CITY BUILDER. WELD THE NIGHT INTO ITS SISTER ICON.
AND LAST SHE OF THE ROYAL BLOOD, UNWATCHED,
NEAR THE LETTER DESK. THERE IS NO WAY OF
REVERSING HER PLEA TO THE REALITY OF THE
NEWSPAPER. HER WORDS FLOWER IN PRINT AT
BREAKFAST, BEFORE THE MAIDSERVANTS SEE THE
PAPER, WHICH WAS PRINTED IN LIME. ALL KINDS OF

BELLS WRING OUTSIDE THE THINKING WALKWAY
WHERE HIS WORDS END IN A PIER. I DON'T KNOW
WHETHER WE WERE HERE BEFORE. IT MAKES NO
DIFFERENCE IF GUARDIAN BANNERS KEEP MILITARY
HOURS IN THE LONG VIEW OF MEN ALONG THE
TOWERS, WHERE WORDS DIE LIKE PRODUCTS HEARING
THEIR ADVERTISING. REMOVE THE COBWEBS. WHITE
MARBLE, WHERE NIGHT'S DISCONNECTED. GOING
HOME TOGETHER. SCREAMING AND YELLING. THE
RUSSIAN TEA ROOM. CAVIAR AND CHAMPAGNE.
WHITEFISH AND SALMON. SHRIMP COCKTAIL. I DON'T
KNOW WHAT THEY WERE DRINKING. POINT IS IN
ANOTHER MOMENT, LOSING MY SISTER. MUCH GRAYER
FALLS, BANISHED IMAGINATION. A LOW FRAME OF
INFERENCES. MESSAGES BY RADIATOR.

RENTED A SCHOOL BUS FOR ME AND MY FRIENDS. WE
MET IN THE SCHOOLYARD WITH OTHERS ARRIVING.
TWO YEARS IN A ROW WE RETURNED TO CRANE'S
BEACH.
AND ONCE ON A BUS DEPARTED INTO GRAVE
IMAGININGS OF DOORS AT ENDS OF LANES BEHIND
WHICH LAY MY UNKNOWN LADY LOVE. ALL OF NEW
ENGLAND MAY HAVE POSSESSED HER.
CHIEFLY THE TITS OF WIVES WHO ARE IGNORED
THROUGHOUT THE TIME OF YEAR. A SECRET WORLD
UNFOLDS IN THE MEMORY OF WHAT CAN BE. GHOSTS
MAY OR MAY NOT BE ABLE TO HAUNT YOU. THIS MOVIE
PORTRAYS THEIR PLIGHT IN A MEDIUM OF LETTERS AS
IT WERE IN ACCORD WITH THE CLASSICAL STRICTURES
OF THE DAY. THE IMPERIUM OF THE INTELLIGENTISTIC
CROP. MR. HAGUE STAYED FAR AWAY IN PROVIDENCE.
THE RETURN OF THE ORPHAN STUNS THE DRAMATIC

CRUX, SHIFTING THE QUEEN, AND PEPPERING THE YALE
REVIEW. NO PEACE IN SUMMER IN THE MARION
MANSION. ALONE ON THE BEACH AT NIGHT. THE DYING
OF THE OCEAN. TRICKS OF STARS. THAT IT SHOULD
STAND ALONE, EXEMPLAR OF SIGNIFICANCE, AS RAINY
AS RAIN, AS WINDY AS WIND, THESE CRISP CERTIFICATES
OF A TIME AND PLACE. FORCED BY SMALL FRAMES INTO
CONFUSIONS OF PROSE, COLOURED, REFRACTIVE, ALIVE
TO SUCH TIMES AS 1945 OR 1943. MUCH NOT
UNDERSTOOD AT THE TIME. FOR LYRIC JOLTS IMAGINE
MY HEART SEPARATED FROM THE STARS, THE ICY
STRINGS OF MY BEST WISHES SHOCKED IN DESIRE AS I
KNEW THEY WOULD BE THEN THE STARS FELL. I WAS
SERVED A NAPKIN IN A RIBBON. ATTACK IN SNOW.
CUISSARS SHAKE SWORDS IN INK. SHIPS DEBARK. THE
FOGHORN BY THE RIVER IS NOT INCOME. BUT THE
MOVIES ARE PLAYING AGAIN AND I WANT TO SEE ONE.
TO BE LET LOOSE UPON THE DARKENED PLANES
WHERE YEAR IS A FIRST BREATH AND UTTERANCE
CALLED BY THE FOREST WHERE NOTHING IS IN PRINT
RADIO SIGNALS GENTLEMEN MAP OUR PROGRESS
AND NOT AN INELUCTABLE LINE
THROUGH THE DEVASTATED PICNICS
OF OUR OWN NATIONAL TREASURE
THE LAND OF OUR FATHERS.
NOW I AM CLOSING THE BOOKSTORE, GEPETTO'S SHOP,
THE LITTLE VIEW ON A CHILD'S TRICKS, PLEASURE FOR
THE SKINNING, A GLIMPSE OF HER IN THE WHITE
BAKERY, GRANDFATHER TOLD ME SO, ON HIS KNEE, ON
HIS WHITE LEATHER ARM CHAIR, SMOKING CIGARS
AND WATCHING ZORRO FROM 45 FEET.
THE CARDS ARE PLAYED. THE DIVINER MUSIC
THUNDERS THROUGH THE PRAYING HOUSE. SISTERS

ARE TWO AUNTS. BROTHER UNMARRIED. ONE WITH HER
SERVANTS. AN EXCEPTIONAL ARTIST. SILENCE IN THE
KITCHEN. QUICK WITH HER WITS. CONVERSANT WITH
WITCHES. I AM NOT ROBERT LOWELL. I HOWEVER GOT
AROUND NEW ENGLAND.
CHAPLIN WHO WINS THE GIRL AND LAUREL AND
HARDY WHO BRING EACH OTHER THE DEAREST
AFFECTION. INTERMINABLY WROUGHT OUT ON A COLD
NIGHT. TURNING TO EACH OTHER FOR LUCK AND
SPIRITS. IN THE END ALL THEY GOT. BUT WHAT
CONFIDENCE THEY INSTILL IN EACH OTHER! LAYING
SIEGE TO RECKLESS MAYHEM. ABBOTT AND COSTELLO
LIVE WHERE SIMPLE CONNECTIONS ALLOW THE MOST
BASIC LIFE TO FLOURISH. SIMPLE ATTITUDES OF
COMEDY ARE ENDEARING IN A STRAIGHT FACE IN
UNLIKELY SITUATIONS. THESE ARE NOT ALL THE
NIGHTS WE STOOD TALKING OUTSIDE THE GARDEN IN
THE CHURCH YARD. THEN I PLANTED ALL MY IDEAS IN
YOUR HEAD AND YOU CAPITULATED UNDER THE STARS.

HER SHAPE IS MAGNIFIED BY THE WINDOW. HER SHADE
TRAVELS THE MINUTES WITH A CIVIC MELANCHOLY.
SHE IS DEFINITELY ELECTRIC IN THE PAUSES OF HER
ATTENTION TO HER NEW SURROUNDINGS, MADE
CONSTANTLY NEW BY HIS ABSENCE. SHE WAS NOT
WRITING AGAIN HOW SHE FELT WHILE HE WAS
ANSWERING HER LETTERS AS THOUGH UNCONCERNED
BY THE BREADTH OF HER REPLIES. IT WAS AN
ADMIXTURE OF INDIFFERENCE AND FAITHLESS HOPE.
OUR AGE ANSWERS NOTHING TO IT. THERE ARE
UNCITED HEROES.

Before

Hypodermic ink
discrete harbour
swirl cellular
receptive concourse
valid station
adhere reversal
disparate nothing
symbol inversion
shadow framework
glass resilience
distance nothing
blank foreshadowing
before present
not returning
isolate distance
blank abstraction
brilliant rim
look returning
echo foreknowledge
know indifference
naval returning
awkward knowledge
something nothing
distance veiling
swift recovery
eternal nothing
dawn prebreaking
not understanding
with preknowing
the foregoing
dawn Pearl Harbour

next to nothing
not yet lifting
stiff and fragile
towards unknowing
or survival
clefts of shadow
left till morning
breakpoint lighting
next to nothing
at the dockend
of your cigarette
pet my nothing
hair and finger
glass and leave
wind breath vocal
radiant spectrum
ink injection
fragile folio
buff past memory
like survival
not yet knowing
back toward knowing
before knowing
what not happened
not yet happened
yet will happen
yet what happened
glass and oval
desk and treasure
eye signature
matrix shadow
feeding blooming
thick tomorrow

steady delible
house and brilliant
light and moving
cloud and flowing
air and eager
diamond stylus
beacon
mask and shadow
indistinct cipher
cell and surface
teleological
annihilation
and distinction
civilization
unpredictable
and predictable
so long afterward
much as always
cease particular

Tonga

Out by the international dateline
where time begins in the earth's atmosphere
as far as can be from any mainland
surrounded by ocean to the southern pole
it's dizzying to catch the ocean breeze
and dizzying to speak with the natives
who are hemmed in without a newspaper
except what we deliver through the air
from Honolulu or Australia
(it's difficult for aircraft just to land
on such a slender strip you might have missed
patrolling vast unrecognizable
wastelands of ocean in a linear motion,
not mentioning there's no place to refuel
beyond Vanuatu or Kiribati,
the Marshall Islands falling in the sea)
and dizzying turned under from the sun
where even satellites refuse to go
and post their differentials to the moon;
we're upside down here, settling into talk
among the grasses, the colonial palace
of the last uncolonized monarchy,
there's tea for you, and tea for me,
and passports for a bindle of currency;
cultural gifts that few will get to see
are removed to the palace of the old king
his friend, his police captain, and his spokesman
is missing at golf, and won't be here today,
making his rounds of confiscations
protecting citizens under the new bill
just last week passed and signed by the old king

permitting no anti-government journalism
no freedom of the press (where we come in,
launching our cutting edge of poetry
like fresh air to selected citizens;
we're going to mount our reputations here
on this quelled insulated friendly isle
friendly to transport of Al-Queda warheads
they didn't know their boats were carrying;
how many international criminals
have found discreet peace here, new identities,
allowing them to contribute to the culture
in little ways, by sponsoring brisk teas
where they respect the monarch's aging wishes
and find a little chore or two to do,
mostly to keep things running pretty smoothly
among the known world's highest literacy
where Tongan, Tongan, Tongan reigns supreme
down to the water, the corrugated shacks
hungry for poetry news from Cambridge, Mass.;
it's dizzying, dizzying, to be cast so far
from any other mainland, closer to the moon
in understanding intersubjectivity.
You tilt the globe to see how far it is
it might fall off, be swept over, or forgotten,
but the monarch has been rich for fifty years,
he's old and stoops, observing with dark shades
his little military exercises
performed with a quaint and pre-Edwardian feel
rag tag as demonstrations in Vancouver
when the English Queen was visiting;
Oh Tonga, Tonga, by your lights no leave
gives me no hope to buy the government,
install myself as king in quiet peace,

for the king is old, must be approaching death,
though his old flunkeys never think of it.
Tonga, Tonga, it's so dizzying
receiving odd supplies from Honolulu
Havana of the west, Pacific haven
for adventurers who've lost their names
but fit in with the slow and daily pace
of the monarch's generosity
I want to live there, far from continents,
close to the dizzying moon and southern pole
where day begins for all the certain earth's
trust in firm numbers, nothing to the sea,
dizzying, dizzying, ready to collapse
from an unvetted critical intrusion,
from Yale's designs to instigate confusion
and spread the latest word to promulgate
incendiary interests on their dripping peace.
So dizzy, dizzy, underneath the world,
spread like a picnic on the ocean,
unrecognizable on any map
on google global or atlas msn,
lost as moon craters or a speck of dust,
hanging upside down in primitive lust
communal and untouchable their ports
the daily delivery by air inspected
for just the sort of cosmopolitan
eastern propaganda, capital
the monarch confiscates or highly taxes
until my surreptitious operation
enlists approval from the CIA
within the bounds of international law
subjected to the monarch's scrutiny;
where nothing escapes the notice of the king.

Oh Tonga Tonga, dizzying education
in primitive charm and ancient rituals
ordained by the half-century's monarchy
at last I'll make my exit to the moon
and touch down in the sub-tropical waters
where no one can find me, where I can't even breath
so rarefied the air swept by the ocean
outside surveillance, beyond the calendar,
like upside down boxes of cereal
I empty on the table, too proud to eat,
marvelling at the direction through earth's center
that leads me to the silent peace of Tonga.
No longer on any map, I'll be myself.
A wise man with an ivy education,
a friend to primitives and government,
advisor to the bankers and the flunkeys
who are the same, in need of better speeches.
So Tonga bring me in, a secret weapon
to increase trade and visibility,
to edit a respectful local paper
with news of the outside world and cutting culture
that cannot hurt the monarch's steady grip
on the compliance of his faithful subjects
but do not hack my emails in the east,
Tonga is mine, the dizzying atmosphere
is what I seek, quite far from any mainland,
adrift in the ocean nearer the southern pole
indifferent to testings on the Marshall Islands
where I shall sit beneath a breadfruit tree
counting the minutes of imagination
and testing the mails to see what can get through
supplies to print my kind of newspaper
which I'll distribute hoping to be king

after researching the better addresses
of my potential allies among the people.
No spyplanes and no spying satellites
will know what I am doing, in the skies
I see reflections of an endless sea
which I maintain shall all belong to me
no matter if the air grows somewhat thin
and coastlines crumble where I make my fortune,
as close to outer space as earth can be.

Elegy in a Windy Rain

I

Obviously your no means yes,
as in no babies,
no text messages,
no trip to Gloucester.
I am always with you
in the graveyard,
where a wind like white stone
carries the feeling of you to me,
through me.
Nothing else matters.
I sit here,
day after day,
following these same shadows
deeper into winter,
your refusals.

How much then
it must have meant
when I accepted you
at face value,
with a little patience.
Nothing meant more to me,
or still does,
than waiting for you
to find out how you feel.
Or to be thrown into blue
written on the sky
at the end of waiting.

II

I love your self control,
and your slow way
of making up your mind.
Thank god.
I think too much,
you worry too much.
I'm so happy for you.
One dreams
of an ideal—
or is dreamed
an ideal.
The latter,
happens rarely,
expects nature
(as if George Washington under attack)
to respond
in a harmonic accordance
with its image.
Which is
established by
(and here his uncle's eyes flickered,
subsuming thrust of futurity long unborn)
observation of pacts.
I laugh and cry and tell you all I feel.
Patience doesn't seem like a big deal.
To be platonically in love
that is to admire as a moviegoer
your reasons for being.
Informing sometimes by opposites
and acts of silence
barring love itself

the weight that's given.
If in the face of codes
old fairy tales
contract old love
it is endurance
in imagination
and fortune defines itself
as a quintessence of beauty,
just possible.
On faith
consent and vows of order
which honor love
are in themselves binding
and substantiate beauty
by what they honor.

III

These winds speak like the heart because
they see in them what they want to see,
undisturbed by any other by definition.
Quieter permanences of lesser consequence
awarded an equality that felt comfortable
in a highly unexpected way.
No wonder then now in October
the month of skeletons and halloween
would I want to hold in my arms
these images like a bunch of fallen leaves.

A naying and a braying,
wild winds are spraying.
In a cold rain
the bare petals
speak the heart.

The Pegasii

Sunlight rests like a package at the door.
Nothing sees. The rich interior
is useless to persons and chronology.
Once when the spring came to our caravan
I'd say the mountain streams ran in her hair.
Let these things rest without a memory.

The Ghosts

Immediately finding themselves dead,
above their fallen bodies
the ghosts watch with astonishment and rage
to see the evening through a lens of fire
as friends and lovers in a strange parade
pass not hearing. Love's own ground
is patient in eternity. The proof
of love is hidden, but familiar.
It was as fresh as spring, in the old life.
To have no idea of the coming change.
Not long ago, the climate's urgencies
sped them to silence. A sense of hope
is what lingers. Each counterpart of ghosts
relives serenity, the daily puzzle
of shadow on shadow, smiles unwinding talk
where everything happens, as proof exists.
How could they have known what it was like?
The violence of a ghost disarranging books.

San Francisco Poems

I

Homage to California

He built his home up on the glittering hill.
I wanted to own the earth. Dear—
I have been struggling a lot
lately with the meaning of my life.
Twenty years later in the history of the world
I return to *languid mysteriousness,*
night blooming jasmine—the scene of this
my youth I had forgotten (ledge)
and the deep darkness of the brightest star—
I swear I remember impossible alcoves
I came up once where the secluding vines
and oriental gardens knew my mind,
in the first days of being steeped in wine.
I loved then. I love now. Love is the same.
It is not possible to love enough
the distant sweetness of this paradise.
Like a museum is the life I watch—
no one can hear me now or see me now—
Aliki Barnstone Ted Walther George Hitchcock
my roommate John and Lawrence who is dead
the ring of dancers circling through the wood
is broken. Forever time begins again.
Life is different. Nothing is the same.
My life is waste. I wanted to own the earth.

Shut out of the twentieth century—
you cannot hear a one of these pressed flowers.
Everything I love spells ALCATRAZ

The headlight through pine needles. The first glimpse
at the bronze lawn piece of the chancellor.
Beneficiaries of their foresight and generosity—
the pioneers who placed our haven here
where life takes place—where love's incipient,
for each one circling the observatory.
It hurts so bad to never speak with you.

II
Homage to Weldon Kees

The variegated coastlines of disjunctive
blue grey technicolor roofs and rain
surmise the cat's walk. Coming on the plane
the thick bouquet of lights was sparkling thicker
than all of twenty years before. You wrote—
I was not there to answer. I was not there.

It is the most I can do to recall
what I'm not even sure was ever real—
gardens that were built before we were born
that seemed to draw us into a lost time,
invitations that were archetypal.
Under that rain it's as if life begins,
and is a thing we never knew before. . .
so wonderful the night must die with it.

III
Starting from Top of Vallejo, Second Night

Then out of the darkness as if with no past
shadow itself turned to shadow not there.
They say the killer walks here every day.

The body hangs where flowers do not care
in the thick thicket turning the same way.
The killer is not reproached; he *is* reproached.
Who would want to litter in San Francisco?
You could get infected, you could die.
I've never heard such silence in my life,
silence of knowing no one and the wind,
the absolute silence of a noisy wind.
Then there are the chimes, they chime ten years
or more. The pearls go over the bridge,
far more worse than being misunderstood.
This is right. This is comeuppance. Reality.

Don't you ever wonder what we missed?
There is a private lookout which was built
behind Coit Tower, an inverted gorge,
thin wood-railed precipice the cat defends.
To hell with how most people are—the roofs
are something else again, a life unlived.
A summer magnified to many years.
This tier of gardens like the heart of man,
maze-like as all appendages of time,
the secret chambers stacked to tantalize,
long passages that open in the brush.
Admit it's sad to know that you will die.
Not only they did, meaning of *before*,
but disappeared into another day
of hallowed plantings and of hallowed stone.

Smell of remembrance! Birds of Florida!
Too much of tourist's tan new leather. Prop
of regeneration. Glen plaid and white slacks.
It hardly makes a difference, but what does

is scattered among the pigeons and the gulls
and the wide gravel of the pier's warehouse,
the tattooed sparkle of the denizens.
See you at Costo. I am parting thus.
One feels so much freer in California.

Divine Rights

The marriage of druids and Romans
write it
I don't even know how to spell it
It is my real birth today Cadwaladr

Why would they marry?
Where is everything
I am the descendent
        of the king
They were protecting
        the son of
                the king
not father
mother

Landis
Mary
The Poet King
I knew all this
I know all this
We must have been
at alliance with the Scottish.
We must have
been at war
with the Irish
        king.
I know these things.
Freud got it right.
But it is a
throwing off
of kings.

The English King.
The English Queen.
And what am I to think of the English queen,
  Elizabeth?
Or the Russian? Familiar as the lion.
Landis, descended from Charlemagne
and twin Dutch admirals?
Or the Scottish princess in the west?

The prophecy told
  me too
  it is true
after I was thirty-five
  I would be king
would regain my
  forgotten kingdom
what this means
  would be revealed
  would be recovered
every time I had my
   hand read
  or my cards told
Now it has come
  on my real day
   of birth

Florence
after Troy
in the confining hour of our winter
How would you be able to know
you were able to be the mother
of the father
of the king?

often assisted by the Scottish

Herb Hillman
Karen Penn
The Holy Experiment
The Sword in the Stone.
Arthur.
Murphy the Irish King?

This is the subject of my poetry.
The Prodigal
The Return
Eliot is sympathetic
What is he to me?
An English prince
and friend of the Welsh King?
Prince Charles
is not the true prince
Was there a son?
Was he the son of Baumgarten?
So then who is Sylvia?
Get out of my castle.
I must go to Wales.
The Faerie Queene is probably
a political commentary on
the lineage of the kings.

When I was five years old
my father
the ward of the king
took me to see
the sword of the lake
splitting the mountain

in an old storm.
la la

They told me
    when I was a child
but I didn't listen
    That's what my
poetry is about
    warmest verse

Musing upon the king my brother's wreck
All I want to know about are kings

These source materials which have lasted longest,
elements of narrative which have stayed the same
longest. Those which have proved most popular.

The Beginning
The Return
The Kitchen
Winter

The insult given Branwen by the Irish
At Guinnion Fort
Arthur bore the image of Mary as his sign
Arcturus or the keeper of the Pole
and thus it was I watched the turn of winter

'I have made a heap of all that i could find' Nennius (Historia Brittonum).
an 'inward wound'
caused by the fear that certain things dear to him should be 'like smoke
        dissipated' (Jones/Nennius, 1951)
i'm guessing in the old cosmology it wd be the first 24 hrs of your actual

                 presence
and i'll attribute that to bertrand russell. these are just notes.—don marquis
                 (1922)

romeo & juliet in berkeley
i was surprised he looked so much like me
disguise him not to look like myself
i remember
he the leviathan in all ages
my father one eyed introduced me to him

(the currence of the past holds own
our against the recogsentiment
or winds like the runner on the shore
away from the sun in a steady
exhalation, at a vast limit of the net
where one exists in a continuum
spreading in a few words
a striding reach up morning—

he's there in all his incarnations)

a date engraved in bronze swings in its chains
under moon under midnight in its bondless bonds
citizenless entropy of stars, what is heard
never viewd as it is, which is as it is not.
Is never as it can be understood,
must by definition answer nothing.
There is no fixing of these loci.

Iwerddon
And they began the banquet and caroused and discoursed.
And when it was more pleasing to them to sleep than to carouse,

they went to rest, and that night Branwen came
Matholwch's bride.
101 Dalmatians

Look in the mirror and you will recall
the white snow of an earlier snow-fall,
how dragon behind rock had threatened rook,
and rains had formed the letters of a book
in which our love is written. Dragon, look.
How queer. The snows of yesteryear are here.

His mother was the daughter of the king
his son her brother and his uncle
who from earliest winter in the kitchen
stood stirring, sifting, towering
in the first curl of the bird's branch
close to him then she made his song
too-wit too-wit tu-lily hi-li-ly tu-wit tu-lo
and interbranched and interladen among the
hyacinth, jack o'whirl o' shadow—
cleaving densities of variant dispersals,
gravities which undercut propensity:
proofs of an undisclosed philately.
Mad's progress relays Delft into land smile
under the textile's firm approval—
Barkowitz', Horovitz' room. Seal approval.
A real anger at dates. Back in dense sandal word—
I see trees, people dancing in the trees,
a formal approval of glass on paper.
Mixing spices like nutmeg and cinnamon.
Looking up the stovepipe for listening last years.
Another one, only as she could have been.

All around us, the snow in the forest.
Snow walking up hill in the forest,
through snow walking up hill.
I was born in the forest.
I was born under the snow.
I would rather be snowed under
than to have to go in to dinner.
I would rather be lost, out of all ear.
Where the ice thunder with its own snow choir.
Where repetitive naming is lost on hard vortex.
Edge

Their darkness is the sleep in her eyes,
before parting.

Tu-wit. And cherry.
Twice cherry. Cherry Street, and cheery
cheery cherry in the song, all along.
A name for marble torsos and a night port,
everything you wrote in the guest book.
A quick way to do the invitations in summer.
The inn I am staying in, and what a bother.
Why you never answered embroidered on the hem of your
sweater.

We were in the mountains. This genius
was in trust to the genius of the forest.
She didn't nothing that she didn't do.
The forest was a game, where I was first
the others were blind, even she my mother
which meant that I was king.
I have seen these things before they happen.
I have seen her bake day into evening,

have seen her bake the forest into evening,
have seen her bake the hour of homecoming.
The birds are details in her narrative,
ingredients recipes get around to having.
Talk is sure word made out of it,
I wouldn't in wind or rain doubt it,
to gather or collect to retell or rerecollect
every word which the father
brought home for him to inspect.

Why then a king
through kinship of a lady?
A virgin birth. Her mother was king,
I do not doubt it,
upon the plains that have no need of naming.
Why then a king took consecrated ground
which was to plainer eye unconsecrated.
Poetry appears to be living.
I heard it strike the sky like keel and thunder
worn into evening like a headline's banter.
I saw it grab my hand like dad in winter.
I walked it home, the sky ripped at the center,
dark merchant hulk. Perpetual, aimless
Leviathan which strikes the heart of time.
My first knowledge of a light in winter.

And when I first returned to town,
nothing shook my memory,
I never saw
the fiery medal
in my own hand,
dull like my days.
Often quoted

early in spring.

Or noticed how my aunt cast
familiar stories against a local past.

The mystery of the virgin mother
it self would appear to have to reappear.
No wonder I didn't get any idea
nor wonder if you too don't get an idea
why none of this was going to simply appear.

I saw this in the absolute symmetry of the outlines
of the bathtub in the apartment in the city in the world
in our time and in all time

The still being there of the resurrection

Time which comes
only to those it visits.

Why then a birth of kings among the females?

And wasn't a female the king of the king?

*   *   *

I've reached territory.

And so I have been protected from marriage.
So too the quelling of the Jewish King.
For Christ must be his Jew
and virgin birth.

I scarcely thought I could return to her.
But remember how I saw myself
under her influence, her double image
binding the speech of then
with speech to come.

The gods are merchants at these dinners.
Maecenas never dilutes his pleasure.

I didn't think they were
serious. But the king was her
and industry among the settlers
lingers without artifact.

You could say she was worth waiting for.
To have seen her
with nothing to spoil the mood
properly in winter.

What made her special
was what she would become.
This was the meaning of the pristine forest
in which you could see the verb repeating,
always showing in numeric mimicry
the voice in the breath
the eye in the imagery

a deep syntax
of auditory visuality:
for that heard of voices
implies the wind has been
where you yourself have.

The newness of those days,
when these were first.

Mixing the silk and sand of salt and sugar
into the flour. Vanilla in the spoon
darkly reflecting her double down the hallway
and upside down up under her apron.
The fortress of butter malleable to time,
beating the retreating oil slick
in the flood of mud.
A sea of milk.

They brought me many designs of Venice silk.
I paid them to stand around, because I was cold.
I wanted to know what they aspired to.
I am his wreck, and him his father's before me.
I like the charge of shadow without name.

And as we watched enacted in the play
he say to her what I to you would say
and she to he what you would say to me,
so we both watch to see how things will end.
You but remember to be a friend.
You greet me unannounced. I come in rain.

And only this remains to be said,
I have come to rid the land of Saxons.

*　　*　　*

Rehearsals of the shadows where you stood
before you have returned into the halls.

And why no mother of a Jewish King
if not a Jewish King within the line?

One Bad King

Then in my grief
I ran into the wood
along the lake's edge,
out of ear shot.
And as I sped
into a gallop
covering much ground,
passing many trees,
not many thoughts
separated from my friends,
who found the tree
of inner light
in which the Welsh King
put his head
before he knew
he was the King,
I saw I was transformed
into a flying horse
and coiled myself
within the forest's nest
to dully sleep
to hear the distant
fall of words
turn into footsteps
of my friends,
covering the woods.
So I would have the apples speak to me.
So I would have this orchard speak to me.

If my blood
could get back in touch with you.
Shannon
Welsh girl with an Irish name.
I am missing from these documents.

Fifty years
after the war
I saw the dead
returning home
on _____ Way.

Then
I was at his house
which was the house
I came from
when I was his
father who I greet.
Under
a rain
the blue city
has the same look
that her eyes had
in her round head
the Scottish Queen.

In that hour
when memory settles
on the evening
darkness its liquid
history of masks,
I quote you
and see the world

as written on the dark sky.
They rearrange
as flame
and fly to conspire
with my father
who is leading us
under the mountain
to the sea beast.
Always outside the room
                in which we talk
above us
            where what must be the roof
is how I see it
if we don't lie and confer,
a mixing of night and day
in which the heart's first urge
speaks, but in words of fire.
They know the night
who came here first
and them I see
in my words' end.

Even then
I knew these things could be without me.
But that I was the King
I saw unknowing.
The first song of spring
in my upbringing.
A curator of lies.
A curator of sleep.
Shut up with your eyes.
I am the King
and I have broken darkness.

Look in the storm.
Look in the barrel.
Look under the mountain.
I am the dragon.

Look where her room
retains the look
of the room of a stranger,
now in the east. Where we began.
I named you then
the Hyacinth girl.
Words that were meant for no other,
as has long been known in the land.

Separating at night.
Ten years in arms.
Talked of as if it happened yesterday.
Cried the ladies,
the vegetables that name themselves.

Mother then
I am your son
the King.

Epilogue

It is youth that understands old age
and your repulsion is but a projection
an image of the loathing you obtain.
I've seen the fall come in and think I shall
follow each leaf that winds about the house
to where you stutter, the end of the tether
where grace walks through the bridal foliage
and no one could mistake you for another.
After that, they are only leaves to burn.
And when the flowers burst upon the rain
the roofs shall keep their solemn gentle witness
far from the young men who travel far
to fill their noses with the autumn air.
Daybreak is decent as awakening.
And love is gentle, though he is no scholar.
What if I filled my notebook with his words
sketched suddenly with no least hesitation
would she return to him when it came fall
or would she sink into a bitter winter
not even counting the blossoms that are gone.
How many times the autumn rain recurs
to wind about the river in the evening
or fall like one great ocean in the dawn.
No matter, he has had enough of her
and leaves his youth in hope of something better.
A drop expresses all the flooding water,
the wind instills the trees with sentiment,
and no one, no one can reverse the patter
of the darkness that's enclosed within.
It stares across the city in the dawn
and cannot wake these shrouds of memory.

Ben Mazer was born in New York City in 1964. His poems have been widely published in international periodicals, including *Fulcrum*, *Verse*, *Harvard Review*, *Jacket*, *Agenda*, *Stand*, *Boston Review*, and *Salt*. His poetry collections include *January 2008* (Dark Sky Books, 2010), and two chapbooks, *The Foundations of Poetry Mathematics* (Cannibal Books, 2008) and *Johanna Poems* (Cy Gist Press, 2007). He is the editor of *Selected Poems of Frederick Goddard Tuckerman* (Harvard University Press, 2010), Landis Everson's *Everything Preserved: Poems 1955-2005* (Graywolf Press, 2006, winner of the first Emily Dickinson Award from the Poetry Foundation), and a forthcoming edition of the poems and critical prose of John Crowe Ransom. He lives in Cambridge, Mass., where he is a contributing editor to *Fulcrum: An Annual of Poetry and Aesthetics*.

www.ingramcontent.com/pod-product-compliance
Lightning Source LLC
LaVergne TN
LVHW041202080426
835511LV00006B/715